The Whimsical Word

CREATION TO ADAM
GENESIS CHAPTERS 1-3

Adaptation by
Brian James Figat

Illustrations by
Dot Dot

May every child learn the wisdom of an elder,
And every adult remember the wonder of youth,
For in this thinking, full of wisdom and whimsy,
We can live out a life of power and truth.

@2025 The Whimsical Word
ISBN: 979-8-218-84474-5
www.whimsicalword.com

"In the beginning..."
is how this Book starts
Before Heaven and Earth
were created in parts.

The Earth was still empty
and dark and all bare
Not a person or animal
was seen living there.

The Spirit of God,
above water deep
Was hovering and waiting,
to awaken its sleep.

"Let there be light!"
is all that He spoke
Then "BAM!"
There was light!
Like a new day awoke.

Lightness and darkness,
and darkness and light
He broke them apart,
one called 'Day',
one called 'Night'.

He looked and He smiled,
this part was done.
It was good. It was perfect.

And that was only Day One.

Then God said aloud,
"Let's split these in two,
A space in between
the waters will do."

This 'Sky' up above,
He now called that 'Space',
And evening. And morning.
"Day Two" was in place.

"Let the waters below this new Heavenly space,
Be gathered together and into one place.
And up from the water, dry land will appear,
We'll call that ground 'Earth', so no water here.

The waters that we collected are 'seas',
Separated so that the land can grow trees,
Plants, fruits and veggies will all contain seeds."
There was evening,
there was morning,
there was beauty,
Day Three.

"Now we need some light up in this expanse,
(The area up where we see the stars dance)
To tell day from night, to have years and days,
To tell apart seasons, we'll see in two ways:

One lesser light, to rule over the night,
So we can still see (but it's not quite as bright)
And one greater glow, so the Earth beams by day."
Now evening, and morning,
Day Four's done, Hurray!

Now God made the seas
to team with great creatures,
And birds that could multiply
(this was one of their features)

Each kept increasing
in keeping with kinds
And filled up the waters
and filled up the skies.

What God saw was good, in the sky and the sea,
And God gave a blessing, it was blessed to be
Fruitful and multiply, to bring forth more life
Evening, then morning -
He was done with Day Five.

The very next day,
He knew what to do,
He brought forth livestock,
and creeping things too,
The marvelous beasts
of the earth came to be,
But was He finished?
Oh no, no sir-ee.

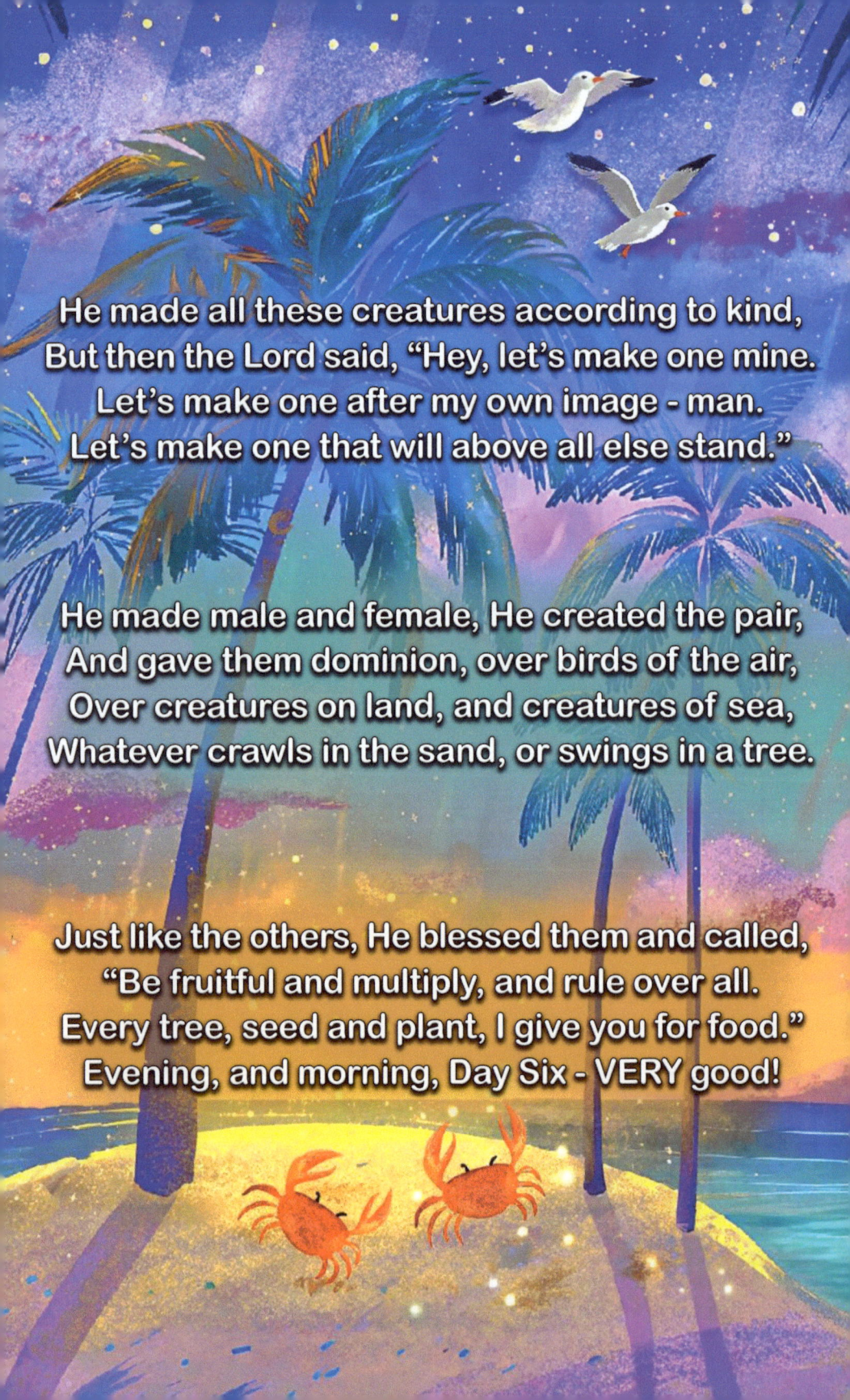

He made all these creatures according to kind,
But then the Lord said, "Hey, let's make one mine.
Let's make one after my own image - man.
Let's make one that will above all else stand."

He made male and female, He created the pair,
And gave them dominion, over birds of the air,
Over creatures on land, and creatures of sea,
Whatever crawls in the sand, or swings in a tree.

Just like the others, He blessed them and called,
"Be fruitful and multiply, and rule over all.
Every tree, seed and plant, I give you for food."
Evening, and morning, Day Six - VERY good!

CHAPTER 2

The Seventh Day came, and all was in place,
So God rested from work, and rested His case
That this day should be Holy,
This day should be blessed,
A lesson that even after Creation, came rest.

Deep in this story, as Earth was formed,
There still were no plants,
and it still hadn't stormed
Because no people were yet there to work
The land or the plants or the herbs or the dirt.

So He set a cool mist to cover the ground,
Up came that water so life could abound,
Then out of the dust, He formed the first man,
And breathed in his nostrils, and new life began.

God planted a garden, just eastward in Eden,
And there placed the man in whom He just breathed in,
And out of the ground, every tree grew,
Pleasant to look at, and good for food, too.

There in the Garden, also there stood,
The Tree of Life, and also of Good
And Evil, a tree that gave knowledge of
Things that God knew, the things of above.

A river flowed out of Eden, a stream,
A river to water the garden so green.
From there it all parted, in four different beds,
In four new directions, four riverheads.

The first, named "Pishon",
and it goes around
a whole land called "Havilah",
where gold filled the ground
This gold was one of the
best that was known,
There also was resin,
and the onyx stone.

A second branch flowed,
this one called "Gihon",
It flowed around Cush
(it was really that long).
The "Tigris", the third,
went east of Asshur,
The forth, called "Euphrates",
you've heard of, I'm sure.

Now God took the man, and placed him in Eden,
To tend to the Garden, to tend and to keep it.

And God gave forth a command to the man,
"You can eat from almost every tree,
but you must understand,
All except one, Good and Evil,
that's totally banned."

And the Lord God said, "It is not good,
For a man to be alone, so I should
Make him a helper, a perfect fit,
Comparable in every way, every bit."

The man chose a name for each of the animals,
Livestock and birds and the wildest of mammals,
But still, no suitable helper was right,
To be found for the man, in whom he could delight.

So God caused the man to fall into a sleep
(And the Creator made sure
that the man's sleep was deep),
Then he took out a rib from the man in that state,
And closed up the opening, and began to create...

A snake, a serpent, the shrewdest of all
Was there in the Garden, and up to her crawled.

And asked:
"Did God really say
that you cannot eat
The fruit from any of
this Garden's trees?"

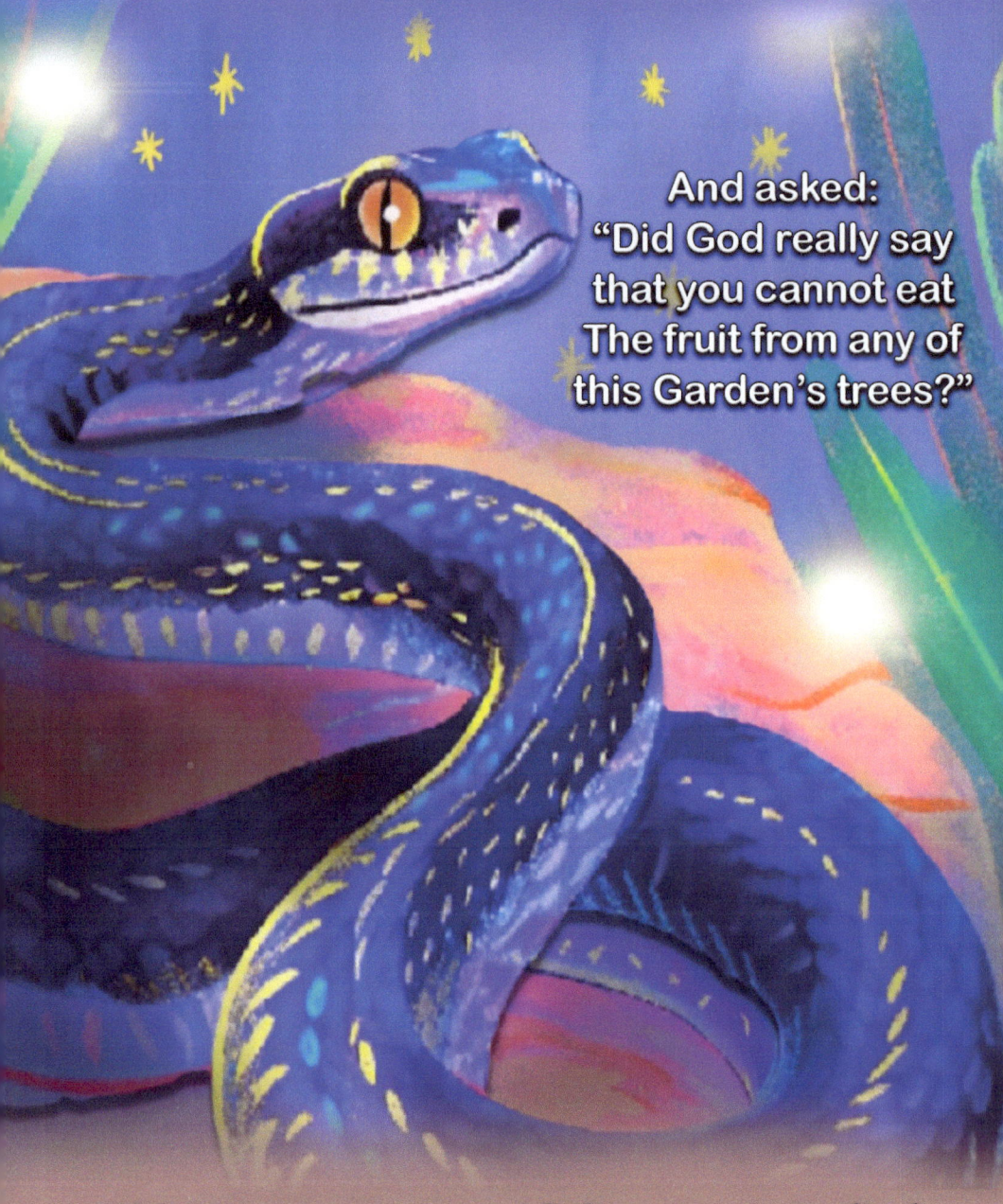

"Of course we may eat," the woman replied,
"Fruit from the trees of this place we reside,
It is only the fruit from the one in the middle,
We cannot eat, or even touch just a little."

"For if we touch it or eat it, then we will die."
And then with quick thought, the serpent replied,
"You won't die, surely God knows
it will open your eyes,
You'll know good from evil,
You'll be like God - wise."

Well, that little thought,
was all that it took,
The woman glanced over
and took in a look,
Of that beautiful tree,
with its beautiful lure,
Delicious,
and she wanted
its wisdom for sure.

So she took it and ate of the fruit of that tree,
She ate of the tree which God said to let be,

She gave to her husband,
and he ate it too,
For why would God
say they could not?

...then they knew.

Right away both their eyes
were now opened wide,
They felt sudden shame,
and now couldn't hide,
They were bare, they were there,
with nothing to cover
So they sowed up some fig leaves
to cover each other.

In the cool of the day, they heard a faint sound,
It was their Lord God, walking around
He was there in the Garden,
so Adam and Eve - they hid!
They hid from the shame of what they both did.

"Where are you Adam?" the Lord God cried out.
And Adam came forth, and said out of his mouth,
"I heard Your voice call, Your voice I did hear,
But because I was naked, I hid out of fear."

"Who told you that you
were naked and bare?
Did you eat of that tree,
that tree over there?
The one tree I told you
Never to eat of?
The one single tree
To not make a meal of?"

"Serpent," the Lord God looked sternly and spoke
The words no one ever would want God to invoke:
"Because you have done this, your cunning deceit,

You are more cursed,

more cursed than all beasts,

"More cursed than all cattle,

more cursed in all ways,

On your belly you'll crawl,
and eat dust all your days.
You'll be a sworn enemy, to her and her line
You'll strike the man's heel,
but your head - won't be fine..."

"Now cursed is the ground, cursed for your sake,
You'll toil and struggle; your sweat, it will take,
You'll work through thistles and thorns for your grain
You'll have bread to eat, but it will take pain.

You'll do this until you return to the ground,
Return to the ground from where you were found.
For remember, I once formed you out of the dust,
To dust you'll return, that is a must."

So Eve was the name Adam chose for his wife,
Since she was the mother, the mother of life,
And now God created them tunics of skin,
And clothed them, and gave them
these skins to dress in.

"They've now become more like Us, more like Me,
They've learned Good and Evil,
their eyes can now see.
So one thing they CAN NOT DO is to take
And eat from the Tree of Life's fruit, for their sake.

For then he would go on and on, live forever."
So God drove the man out of Eden, so he'd never
Eat of that tree and have eternity awaken,
He'll now till the ground from which he was taken.

www.ingramcontent.com/pod-product-compliance
Lightning Source LLC
Chambersburg PA
CBHW041809040426
42449CB00001B/36